ROUTE 66 AN ACCESSIBLE GUIDE TO AMERICA'S MOST ICONIC ROAD TRIP

Route 66 An Accessible Guide to America's Most Iconic Road Trip

Amy Tarpein

Mug Memoirs

Contents

Foreword

There are people who travel the world to collect miles. And then there are people who travel the world to collect meaning.

Amy Tarpein is the latter. I have watched her, as a mother, an advocate, a storyteller, and a leader, turn the simple act of traveling with her "mini-humans" into a movement that has changed how families, destinations, and entire industries think about accessibility.

She does not approach travel as a luxury. She approaches it as a birthright one that belongs to every family, every child, everybody, every ability. This book is not just a guide to Route 66. It is a testament to what happens when love becomes courage, and courage becomes action.

Amy writes from lived experience, the kind that cannot be faked, taught, or borrowed. She writes from the front lines of caregiving, from the quiet moments in hospital rooms, from the joyful chaos of traveling alone with five children, from the deep well of resilience that comes from raising a medically complex child in a world that wasn't built with him in mind. And yet, she never writes with bitterness. She writes with hope.

She writes with the kind of clarity that only comes from walking through fire and choosing, again and again, to build something beautiful from the ashes. She writes with humor, humility, and a tenderness that will stay with you long after you close the book.

What you hold in your hands is more than a travel guide. It is a companion. A mentor. A reminder that the world is still full of wonder and that every family deserves to experience it.

Amy doesn't just show you Route 66. She shows you what it means to belong on the road. And once you see the Mother Road through her eyes, you will never see it the same way again.

-A fellow traveler who has been changed by her work

For Elijah and the mini-humans who taught me that
adventure is not measured in miles, but in moments of
courage, connection, and joy.

And for every family who has ever been told what they
can't do. May this book remind you of everything you
can.

Prologue

Where the Road Begins, Before the Road Begins

Every journey has two beginnings.

There's the moment your wheels touch the pavement, the official start, the one marked by a sign, a map, or a mile marker. And then there's the quieter beginning, the one that happens long before you ever pack a bag.

For me, the real beginning of this journey happened on a shoreline.

I was standing at the edge of the ocean, holding a baby who had already taught me more about resilience than most people learn in a lifetime. Elijah's diagnosis had rearranged my world not by breaking it, but by revealing how much strength, softness, and community it could hold. I made a promise that day: that we would not shrink our lives to fit the limits others imagined for us. That we would travel, explore, and experience the world together, not someday, but now.

Route 66 became the symbol of that promise. Not because it's easy. Not because it's perfect. But because it's real.

It's a road built by dreamers, travelers, families, workers, immigrants, artists, and everyday people who believed in possibility. It's a road that holds history and heartbreak, joy and grit, neon and dust. It's a road that invites you to slow down, look around, and remember that life is not meant to be rushed.

This book is not just a guide. It's a story, our story, woven into the Mother Road.

It's a love letter to accessible family travel. A testament to resilience. A celebration of small towns and big skies. A reminder that adventure belongs to all of us.

And it begins, as all good journeys do, with a single step or roll toward something new.

How to Use This Book

A Guide for Your Own Journey

This book is part travel guide, part memoir, part lived-experience companion for families, caregivers, and travelers of all abilities. You can read it cover to cover like a story, or you can use it as a practical tool while planning your own Route 66 adventure.

Here's how to get the most out of it:

1. READ IT LIKE A JOURNEY.

Each chapter follows the natural east-to-west flow of Route 66, with emotional transitions that mirror the rhythm of the road.

2. USE THE STOPS AS A GUIDE, NOT A CHECKLIST.

Every stop included here is accessible, meaningful, and family-friendly. But you don't have to see them all. Choose what fits your pace, your needs, and your joy.

3. LOOK FOR THE ACCESSIBILITY NOTES WOVEN INTO THE NARRATIVE.

Instead of clinical checklists, accessibility is integrated into the storytelling because that's how it shows up in real life.

4. USE THE MEMORY TABLES TO CAPTURE YOUR OWN STORY.

Each chapter ends with a space for your memories. Fill them in as you go. This book becomes more valuable when your story lives inside it.

5. REFLECT AS YOU TRAVEL.

The reflection questions at the end of each chapter are invitations, not assignments. Use them to deepen your experience, connect with your family, or simply pause and breathe.

6. LET THIS BOOK BE A COMPANION, NOT A RULE BOOK.

Route 66 is not about perfection. It's about presence. Let the road surprise you. Let the moments unfold. Let yourself be changed.

Author's Note

The Mini- Humans at Desert View Tower, Grand Canyon

Why This Book Exists

I didn't write this book because Route 66 is famous. I wrote it because Route 66 is human.

It's a road built by people who believed in possibility and traveled by people who needed it. Families. Dreamers. Workers. Wanderers. Caregivers. Children. People searching for something. People running from something. People running toward something.

When I began traveling with Elijah and his siblings, I realized how few resources existed for families like ours families navigating accessibility, medical needs, sensory needs, mobility devices, and the emotional weight of traveling with a child who requires more.

I wanted to change that.

This book is my way of saying: You belong on this road. Your family belongs in these stories. Your joy belongs in these places.

Every chapter blends practical guidance with lived experience, the kind you only learn by rolling through the world with a medically complex child and a heart full of hope.

I hope this book helps you plan. I hope it helps you dream. But more than anything, I hope it helps you feel seen.

Because the road is wide enough for all of us. And adventure belongs to everyone.

1

Illinois

BEGINNINGS & ANTICIPATION

Where the Mother Road whispers its first invitation.

There's something sacred about beginnings. They hold a kind of electricity, the quiet hum of possibility, the soft breath before a story unfolds. Illinois is where Route 66 takes its very first step, and for so many families, dreamers, wanderers, and weary souls, this is where the road begins to change them.

For us, Illinois was the place where anticipation lived. Where the kids pressed their faces to the windows, where the mini-humans buzzed with excitement, where the air felt thick with the promise of adventure. The start of Route 66 isn't just a sign on a pole, it's a doorway. A threshold. A moment where you decide to step into something bigger than yourself.

And Illinois welcomes you with open arms.

It gives you skyscrapers and sculpture gardens, quiet parks and bustling museums, retro diners and roadside nostalgia. It gives you the first taste of what the Mother Road does best: it slows you down, invites you in, and reminds you that the journey is just as important as the destination.

Cloud Gate "The Bean"

1. Route 66 Start Sign & Cloud Gate ("The Bean"), Chicago

Every great journey deserves a great beginning, and Chicago delivers one with style. Standing beneath the **Route 66 Start Sign**, you feel the weight of history and the thrill of possibility. The sidewalk is wide and smooth, the city hums around you, and for a moment, you're part of something timeless, a tradition of travelers who stood right here, took a breath, and stepped into the unknown.

Just a short roll away, **Cloud Gate** rises like a silver dream. Kids love seeing themselves reflected in its curved surface, adults marvel at the engineering, and Elijah's siblings always race to find the funniest distorted reflection. The pathways are accessible, the atmosphere is joyful, and the sculpture itself feels like a symbol of what's ahead: a chance to see yourself and the world from a new angle.

Millennium Park surrounds you with gardens, art, and open space. It's the perfect place to let the excitement settle in your bones before the road begins to unwind beneath your wheels.

2. The Art Institute of Chicago

Stepping into the **Art Institute** feels like stepping into a thousand different worlds at once. Monet's soft colors, Van Gogh's swirling skies, O'Keeffe's bold lines, each gallery invites you to slow down, breathe, and let beauty wash over you.

The museum is wonderfully accessible: step-free entrances, elevators, wide galleries, tactile exhibits, audio guides, and free wheelchairs. It's a place where everyone can participate in the wonder.

One of our favorite moments was standing in front of **American Gothic**, the kids giggling as they tried to mimic the stern expressions. Art has a way of grounding you in the present while connecting you to the past, a perfect metaphor for Route 66 itself.

The Mini-humans at American Gothic House in Eldon IA

3. Grant Park

Grant Park is Chicago's front yard, wide, welcoming, and full of life. Smooth paths wind past gardens, sculptures, and the iconic **Buckingham Fountain**, where water dances against the skyline.

It's a place where families picnic, where travelers stretch their legs, where kids chase bubbles, and adults soak in the sun. The accessible restrooms, level walkways, and open spaces make it easy for everyone to enjoy.

As the sun sets and the city lights begin to glow, Grant Park becomes a soft, magical place, a reminder that even in the heart of a bustling city, there is room to breathe.

4. Lou Mitchell's Restaurant

A Chicago institution and a Route 66 classic, **Lou Mitchell's** feels like stepping into a warm memory. The smell of coffee, the clatter of plates, the friendly staff who treat you like family, it's the kind of place where stories begin.

The layout is accessible, the seating flexible, and service animals are welcomed with genuine hospitality. And the food? Pure comfort. Fluffy pancakes, crispy bacon, omelets, fresh-squeezed juice, and complimentary donut holes that make the kids' eyes light up.

It's the perfect send-off meal before hitting the open road.

5. Harvester Park, Burr Ridge

A playground that feels like a love letter to Route 66. Kids climb a 30-foot Chicago skyscraper, splash in water features, and explore roadside-themed structures that spark imagination and laughter.

The park blends nostalgia with play, offering accessible paths, sports courts, wetlands, nature stations, and picnic areas. It's a joyful stop, one that reminds you that travel isn't just about seeing new places, but about creating new memories.

6. Berwyn Murals (Former Spindle Site)

Though the famous **Berwyn Spindle** is gone, its spirit lives on through vibrant murals that celebrate Route 66's quirky past. Smooth sidewalks and accessible transit make it easy to explore the artwork, each mural telling a story of creativity, community, and the ever-evolving Mother Road.

It's a quick stop, but a meaningful one, a reminder that even when landmarks disappear, their stories remain.

7. Rialto Square Theatre, Joliet

Walking into the **Rialto Square Theatre** feels like stepping into a dream. Marble columns, crystal chandeliers, sweeping staircases, it's opulence wrapped in history.

The theatre is wonderfully accessible, with elevators, wheelchair seating, assistive listening devices, and spacious restrooms. The staff goes above and beyond to make every guest feel welcome.

Whether you're catching a show or simply admiring the architecture, the Rialto is a breathtaking stop that celebrates the beauty of shared experiences.

8. Joliet Prison Park

Famous from movies and TV, **Joliet Prison Park** offers guided tours that bring its dramatic history to life. Smooth paths, accessible parking, and thoughtful accommodations make it easy for everyone to explore.

The towering limestone walls and echoing stories remind you that history is not just dates and facts, it's people, choices, and the passage of time.

9. Gemini Giant, Wilmington

One of Route 66's most beloved icons, the **Gemini Giant** stands tall and proud, welcoming travelers with his space-age charm. The viewing area is flat and accessible, with picnic tables nearby for a quick rest.

It's a simple stop, but one that fills you with nostalgia and delight, the kind of moment that makes Route 66 unforgettable

10. Polk-a-Dot Drive-In, Braidwood

A retro diner bursting with color, character, and classic Americana. Elvis, Marilyn, jukeboxes, murals, it's a joyful explosion of nostalgia.

Accessible pathways, wheelchair-friendly picnic tables, and a welcoming staff make it easy for everyone to enjoy. And the food? Burgers, fries, shakes, pure, delicious fun.

11. Ambler's Texaco Gas Station, Dwight

A beautifully restored station that now serves as a visitor center. Step-free entrances, wide doors, accessible restrooms, and friendly staff make it a comfortable and charming stop.

Vintage pumps and signs outside offer perfect photo opportunities, while the picnic area invites you to slow down and savor the moment.

12. Illinois Route 66 Hall of Fame & Museum, Pontiac

A treasure trove of Route 66 history, filled with memorabilia, classic cars, murals, and stories that bring the Mother Road to life. Accessible parking, elevators, wide paths, and helpful staff make it easy to explore.

The giant Route 66 shield mural outside is a must-see, a perfect backdrop for a family photo.

13. Murals on Main Street, Pontiac

Colorful, creative, and full of life, these murals transform the town into an open-air gallery. Wide sidewalks, curb cuts, benches, and nearby parking make it easy to enjoy at your own pace.

Each mural tells a story of community, history, and the enduring spirit of Route 66.

14. Funk's Grove Maple Sirup, Shirley

A sweet, historic stop where maple "sirup" is made with love and tradition. Accessible paths, helpful staff, and a charming shop make it a delightful visit.

The aroma of maple fills the air, and the surrounding grove feels peaceful, a reminder that the simplest moments often become the sweetest memories.

15. Lincoln's Home National Historic Site, Springfield

A beautifully preserved neighborhood where Abraham Lincoln once lived. Accessible paths, tactile exhibits, guided tours, and shaded benches make it a meaningful, inclusive experience.

Walking or rolling through the streets, you feel connected to history in a way that's both grounding and inspiring.

After your tour, take a leisurely stroll through the beautifully landscaped grounds. The serene environment, dotted with benches and shaded by mature trees, invites you to pause and reflect on the significance of this historic setting. For those interested in delving deeper into history, the nearby presidential library and museum offer a wealth of information and interactive exhibits that bring Lincoln's era to vivid life.

16. Cozy Dog Drive-In, Springfield

Home of the original hot dog on a stick, Cozy Dog is a Route 66 classic. Accessible parking, step-free entry, spacious seating, and friendly staff make it a welcoming stop.

The walls are covered in memorabilia, the food is delicious, and the atmosphere is pure Americana. They're still serving up the original batter recipe that Ed Waldmire created way back in 1946, and it's as delicious as ever! As the birthplace of the original hot dog on a stick, Cozy Dog continues to delight taste buds with Ed's homemade chili, spiced with his special Cozy Dog chili blend. This isn't just a meal, it's a nostalgic journey back to the golden days of road trip dining!

Route 66 Drive-In Springfield IL

17. Route 66 Drive-In Theater, Springfield

A magical place where movies meet starlight. Accessible parking, smooth paths, and a nostalgic atmosphere make it a perfect family night out.

Tune your radio, settle in, and let the glow of the screen carry you into the past.

18. The Ariston Café, Litchfield

One of the oldest restaurants on Route 66, the **Ariston Café** is a warm, welcoming stop filled with history and hospitality. Accessible entrances, flexible seating, large-print menus, and attentive staff make it easy for everyone to enjoy.

The food is comforting, the atmosphere cozy, and the sense of tradition unmistakable.

There's a moment as you cross the Mississippi River where the skyline fades behind you and the Gateway Arch rises ahead, a silver curve against the sky, welcoming you into Missouri.

The river beneath you feels symbolic. A crossing. A threshold. A quiet shift from anticipation to momentum.

Illinois was the spark. Missouri is the flame.

As you roll across the bridge, you feel the road settle into your bones. The kids lean toward the windows. The air changes. The journey deepens. You're no longer standing at the beginning, you're in it now, moving forward, carried by the rhythm of the Road.

And somewhere between the riverbanks, you realize: You're not just traveling west. You're traveling inward, toward connection, toward presence, toward something you didn't know you needed.

Capture Your Favorite Moments in Illinois

Memory	Route 66 Location	What Happened	Who You Were With	Why It Stuck With You
1				
2				
3				
4				
5				

Illinois Reflection Questions

Beginnings & Anticipation

- What did the start of Route 66 stir in you excitement, nerves, hope, curiosity
- Which Illinois moment felt like the true beginning of your journey
- How did the blend of city energy and small-town charm shape your first impressions
- What conversations or connections set the tone for the miles ahead
- How did Illinois remind you that every adventure begins with a single step or roll

2

Missouri

MOMENTUM & DISCOVERY

Where the road begins to shift, and the journey starts to feel real.

Crossing from Illinois into Missouri feels like Route 66 is finally exhaling as if the road itself is settling into its rhythm. The skyline of St. Louis rises ahead, the Mississippi glimmers beneath the bridges, and the Mother Road begins to reveal her personality: bold, quirky, historic, and full of heart.

Missouri is where momentum builds. Where the excitement of beginning transforms into the joy of discovery. Where the road starts to feel like a companion, steady, winding, full of surprises.

For families, Missouri is a treasure chest. For accessibility-minded travelers, it's a place that shows what thoughtful design can look like. And for anyone carrying a story or a child, or a hope, or a burden, Missouri offers space to breathe, explore, and be surprised.

St. Louis Union Station Soda Fountain

19. Chain of Rocks Bridge, Madison

There's something magical about stepping onto a bridge that once carried thousands of travelers westward. The **Chain of Rocks Bridge**, with its mile-long span and quirky 22-degree bend, feels like a portal, a place where the past and present meet in the middle of the Mississippi River.

The wide, smooth path makes it easy for wheelchairs, scooters, and strollers to glide across. The river moves slowly beneath you, the breeze carries the scent of water and cottonwood, and interpretive signs share stories of the bridge's long life.

It's peaceful. It's grounding. It's a reminder that every journey is built on the paths others have taken before us.

20. Route 66 State Park, Eureka

Route 66 State Park is a breath of fresh air, literally. Wide board-walks, smooth trails, and open landscapes invite you to slow down and reconnect with nature. The visitor center, housed in a restored roadhouse, offers accessible exhibits that celebrate the history of Times Beach and the Mother Road.

Families picnic under the trees. Kids run/roll along the paths. Elijah's siblings love watching the river drift by. And for caregivers, parents, and travelers who need a moment of calm, this park offers a gentle pause in the journey.

21. Ted Drewes Frozen Custard, St. Louis

Some places become iconic not because they're fancy, but because they're beloved. **Ted Drewes** is one of those places.

The smooth, step-free path to the ordering window, the accessible outdoor seating, the friendly staff, everything about this stop feels welcoming. And the custard? Thick, creamy, nostalgic. A treat that makes kids giggle and adults close their eyes for just a second longer.

As the sun sets and the neon glows, Ted Drewes becomes a tiny celebration on the side of the road, a reminder that joy often comes in simple, sweet moments

22. Gateway Arch & Museum, St. Louis

The **Gateway Arch** rises like a silver ribbon against the sky, a symbol of westward dreams and the courage to keep going. While the tram to the top isn't accessible for wheelchairs or strollers, the grounds and museum offer more than enough wonder to make this stop unforgettable.

The museum is fully accessible, with ramps, elevators, tactile exhibits, audio guides, and assistive listening devices. Kids love the interactive displays. Adults appreciate the history. And everyone feels the weight of the stories that shaped America's westward expansion.

Even from the ground, the Arch inspires awe, a reminder that you don't have to climb to great heights to feel lifted.

23. St. Louis Union Station

Once a bustling train station, now a vibrant hub of entertainment, **St. Louis Union Station** is a place where history and modern joy intertwine. The aquarium, the Ferris wheel, the restaurants, the light shows, everything is designed with accessibility in mind.

Wide pathways. Elevators. Accessible restrooms. Sensory accommodations. Staff who go out of their way to help.

It's a place where families can explore together, where kids can wander safely, and where the echoes of the past blend beautifully with the laughter of the present.

Alice Clock At Adventures of Intrigue in St. Louis MO

24. Adventures of Intrigue, St. Louis

This open-concept escape room is a playful surprise along the Missouri stretch of Route 66. As the only **KultureCity-certified** escape room in the region, it offers sensory-friendly options, wheelchair accessibility, and a staff that genuinely wants every visitor to feel included.

The rooms are imaginative and interactive, inviting families to work together, laugh together, and get lost in the story. It's a reminder that adventure doesn't always require miles, sometimes it just requires curiosity.

25. Missouri History Museum, St. Louis

The **Missouri History Museum** is where stories come alive. Step-free entrances, elevators, wide galleries, and accessible restrooms make it easy for everyone to explore.

The exhibits are rich and engaging, from civil rights to Route 66 to the everyday lives of Missourians across generations. Quiet areas and sensory-friendly options offer comfort for those who need it.

It's a place to learn, reflect, and connect, a reminder that history is not just something we study, but something we carry.

26. Meramec Caverns, Stanton

Descending into **Meramec Caverns** feels like stepping into another world. Cool air wraps around you. The echo of dripping water fills the chambers. Light dances across ancient formations that have been growing, slowly and silently, for millions of years.

While some pathways are steep or narrow, the staff are attentive and compassionate. They communicate clearly about what to expect, offer alternative routes when possible, and provide accessible viewing areas so everyone can experience the magic of the caverns.

They don't rush you. They don't make assumptions. They simply meet you where you are, a gift for families traveling with mobility devices or sensory needs.

It's a stop filled with wonder, a reminder that beauty exists both above and below the surface, waiting for those willing to explore.

27. Wagon Wheel Motel, Cuba

The **Wagon Wheel Motel** is one of the oldest continuously operating motels on Route 66, and one of the most lovingly restored. Its stone cottages, glowing neon, and peaceful pathways feel like a gentle embrace from the past.

Accessible rooms feature widened doorways, step-free entrances, and thoughtful amenities that make the stay comfortable for travelers of all abilities. The property is quiet at night, with soft lighting and a sense of calm that settles over the courtyard.

It's the kind of place where you sit outside your room, breathe in the evening air, and feel grateful for the road beneath you. A place where time slows down just enough for you to rest.

28. Route 66 Museum, Lebanon

Inside the Lebanon library sits a delightful surprise: a vibrant, immersive **Route 66 Museum** that feels like stepping into a time capsule. Vintage cars, recreated streetscapes, neon signs, and nostalgic displays fill the space with color and charm.

The museum is fully accessible, with step-free entrances, wide aisles, and exhibits set at comfortable viewing heights. Staff are warm, knowledgeable, and eager to share stories, the kind of people who make history feel alive.

It's a stop that invites you to linger, to wander slowly, and to imagine the Mother Road as it once was.

29. Fantastic Caverns, Springfield

Fantastic Caverns is one of the most accessible natural wonders on Route 66, a cave you can explore **without leaving your seat**. Visitors roll or walk directly onto a tram that carries you through the cavern's chambers, making it a rare and inclusive experience for travelers with mobility challenges.

The narration is available in multiple formats. Assistive listening devices are offered. Staff are patient, kind, and deeply committed to accessibility.

The cave itself is peaceful and awe-inspiring. Soft lighting reveals delicate formations. The air is cool and still. And the ride-through format allows everyone, kids, adults, wheelchair users, caregivers, to share the wonder together.

It's a reminder that nature belongs to all of us.

Meeting A Giraffe

30. Wild Animal Safari Park, Strafford

This drive-through wildlife adventure is pure joy. From the comfort of your vehicle, you can see giraffes up close, watch zebras wander by, and even pet bison and other animals that approach your window with gentle curiosity.

Accessible restrooms, parking, and guided tour options make it easy for families of all abilities to enjoy the experience. Kids squeal with delight. Adults snap photos. And the animals roam freely, reminding you that the world is full of wild, beautiful surprises.

It's a stop that brings out the child in everyone

Sage advice: do not trust Gypsy the camel! She is a little chaotic and likes to steal from your car!

31. Rutledge-Wilson Farm Park, Springfield

This 207-acre farm park is a celebration of accessibility, inclusion, and simple joys. Wide paths wind through barns, gardens, and open fields. Adaptive bicycles allow more visitors to explore the grounds. Sensory-friendly events create space for families who need a gentler pace.

The kids love the barn animals. Adults appreciate the peaceful trails and shaded seating. And everyone feels welcome, a testament to the park's commitment to community.

It's a place where you can slow down, breathe deeply, and reconnect with the land.

32. Red Oak II, Carthage

Created by artist Lowell Davis, **Red Oak II** is a whimsical, lovingly crafted village that feels like stepping into a storybook. Gravel roads, restored buildings, sculptures, and Americana charm fill the landscape.

It's quiet, quirky, and full of heart, a place where imagination and nostalgia meet. While it might appear to be an old ghost town, don't be fooled, it's a lively, beautifully recreated historic village where nostalgia dances hand-in-hand with creativity. The artist, Lowell Davis, has infused his heart and soul into every corner of Red Oak II, making it a testament to his passion for preserving history and creativity.

33. Route 66 Neon Park, St. Robert

A glowing tribute to the neon era of Route 66, this park features restored signs that light up the night like a celebration. Smooth pathways, accessible parking, and benches make it easy for everyone to enjoy.

As the signs flicker to life, the whole space feels magical, a reminder that the Mother Road has always been a little bit electric.

34. Route 66 Car Museum, Springfield

With more than 70 classic and rare vehicles, the **Route 66 Car Museum** is a paradise for car lovers. Wide aisles, clear signage, and accessible galleries make it easy to explore at your own pace.

The kids marvel at the shiny chrome. Adults reminisce about cars they once owned, or wished they had. And the staff are always ready with a story.

It's a joyful stop that sparks conversations across generations.

35. Wonders of Wildlife National Museum & Aquarium, Springfield

One of the most immersive wildlife attractions in the country, Wonders of Wildlife is designed with accessibility at its core. Wheelchair-friendly paths, elevators, tactile displays, audio tours, captioned videos, and sensory-friendly hours ensure that every visitor can engage fully.

The exhibits are breathtaking, from underwater tunnels to lifelike dioramas that feel like stepping into another world. It's educational, emotional, and deeply moving.

A reminder of the beauty and fragility of the natural world.

36. History Museum on the Square, Springfield

This museum brings Springfield's past to life with interactive exhibits, accessible galleries, quiet hours, and sensory kits for visitors who need them.

It's engaging and thoughtful, with stories that connect the city's history to the broader narrative of Route 66. Every visitor is welcomed, included, and encouraged to explore.

A place where history feels alive.

37. Route 66 Rocker, Fanning

Once the world's largest rocking chair, this towering roadside attraction still delights travelers. Accessible paths and nearby parking make it easy to enjoy.

It's quirky, fun, and perfect for photos, a reminder not to take the journey too seriously.

38. Devil's Elbow, Pulaski County

A scenic stretch of Route 66 with breathtaking views of the Big Piney River. Accessible pull-offs allow everyone to enjoy the landscape.

It's peaceful, nostalgic, and full of natural beauty, a moment to pause and breathe.

39. Stonehenge Replica, Rolla

A fascinating granite replica created with waterjet technology. Accessible paths and interpretive signs make it an easy and educational stop.

It's unexpected, artistic, and a little bit mysterious, just like Route 66 itself.

Uranus Fudge Factory

40. Uranus Fudge Factory, St. Robert

A quirky, colorful, joy-filled stop where humor and nostalgia collide. Accessible paths, restrooms, and parking make it easy to explore the candy shop, museum, and photo ops.

It's silly. It's fun. It's Route 66 at its most playful.

41. Route 66 Welcome Center, Joplin

41. Route 66 Welcome Center, Joplin: Stop by the Joplin Route 66 Visitor Center, where staff will help you find the area's hidden treasures, share Joplin's history, and give you inside information on the Four States area.

View historic Joplin photos, take a tour of key Route 66 icons through the Route 66 gallery, and learn about the murals located in the historic City Hall. The Visitor Center is located in historic downtown Joplin in the former Newman's Department Store.

There's a moment, just west of Joplin, where Missouri begins to loosen its grip, and Kansas rises to meet you. It's not marked by a grand sign or a dramatic shift in scenery. It's quieter than that, a gentle exhale from the road, a soft turning of the page.

This border feels different from the others.

Maybe it's because Missouri is where the journey gains momentum, where the excitement of beginning becomes the rhythm of discovery. Maybe it's because Kansas, with its short but powerful stretch, reminds you that meaning isn't measured in miles. Or maybe it's because this is the point where the road starts to feel personal.

As you leave Missouri, you carry with you the glow of neon, the echo of caverns, the laughter from diners, the stillness of river overlooks, and the kindness of strangers who treated you like family. You carry the weight of history, the bridges, the museums, the stories of resilience and reinvention.

And then, almost without noticing, you cross into Kansas.

The landscape opens. The sky stretches. The road narrows into something intimate and tender. It feels like the Mother Road is leaning in, whispering, *"Slow down. Pay attention. This part matters."*

For families traveling with medically complex children, this border can feel symbolic. Missouri is the chapter where you find your rhythm, where you learn what works, what doesn't, what you need, and how to breathe through the unexpected. Kansas is where you begin to trust yourself. Where you realize you're not just surviving the journey, you're living it.

There's a quiet beauty in that.

Crossing into Kansas, you feel a shift, not in the scenery, but in yourself. A softening. A settling. A sense that you're exactly where you're meant to be.

The road ahead may be short, but it's full of heart. And sometimes, the smallest stretches hold the biggest truths.

Capture Your Favorite Moments in Missouri

Memory	Route 66 Location	What Happened	Who You Were With	Why It Stuck With You
1				
2				
3				
4				
5				

Missouri Reflection Questions

Momentum & Discovery

- What moment in Missouri made the journey feel real for you?
- How did the blend of history, nature, and nostalgia shape your experience?
- Which stop surprised you the most and why?
- How did Missouri invite you to slow down, explore, or connect?
- What conversations or memories from this stretch will you carry forward?

3

Kansas

SMALL MOMENTS WITH BIG MEANING

Exploring the Hidden Gems of Route 66 in Kansas

Kansas may claim only **13.2 miles** of Route 66, but don't let its size fool you, this short stretch is overflowing with charm, history, and heart. As the Mother Road winds through **Baxter Springs, Riverton, and Galena,** travelers discover a collection of small-town treasures that capture the spirit of Route 66 in the most unexpected ways. These stops are welcoming, accessible, and rich with stories that remind you why even the smallest moments on the road can leave the biggest impressions.

Tow Mater Galena, KS

42. Galena Mining & Historical Museum, Galena

Step inside this charming museum and you'll feel the heartbeat of Galena's mining past. Housed in a former railroad depot, the **Galena Mining & Historical Museum** is filled with artifacts, mineral samples, mining equipment, and even a few vintage cars with stories worth asking about.

The layout is accessible and easy to navigate, and the staff greets visitors with genuine warmth. Exhibits highlight the grit, resilience, and tight-knit community that defined Galena's mining era. Interactive displays and knowledgeable docents bring the town's history to life, offering a deeper understanding of how mining shaped the region.

Beyond the mining exhibits, the museum serves as a lively hub for local culture, hosting events and celebrating the heritage of this proud Route 66 town. Whether you're a history buff or simply curious, this stop offers a meaningful glimpse into Galena's past, and its place along the Mother Road.

43. Cars on the Route, Galena

If you're a fan of Pixar's *Cars*, this stop is pure joy. **Cars on the Route**, located in a restored 1934 Kan-O-Tex service station, is home to **Tow Tater**, the real-life inspiration for Tow Mater. It's a must-visit for families, movie lovers, and anyone craving a fun, nostalgic photo op.

The retro diner-style shop is filled with Route 66 memorabilia, souvenirs, and vintage vehicles that celebrate the classic spirit of the open road. It's cheerful, colorful, and guaranteed to bring out your inner kid.

Gearheads, Galena, KS

44. Gearheads, Galena

Located in a beautifully restored **1939 Texaco station**, Gearheads is part souvenir shop, part museum, and part Kansas' only official Route 66 Tourist Information Center. It's quirky, welcoming, and packed with personality.

Inside, you'll find a towering Big A statue, a Betty Boop figure, a massive American flag mural made entirely from Kansas license plates, and a surprisingly photogenic bathroom (yes, get a picture!)

Gearheads is committed to accessibility, ensuring every traveler feels welcome. Friendly staff is always eager to share stories, offer tips, and point you toward other hidden gems along Kansas' short but mighty stretch of Route 66.

45. Rainbow Bridge, Baxter Springs

The **Rainbow Bridge** is a rare treasure: the last remaining single-span concrete Marsh arch bridge on Route 66. Built in 1923, it's a graceful piece of engineering that invites you to slow down and savor the moment.

Walk or roll across its smooth surface and take in the peaceful views of Brush Creek below. Surrounded by lush greenery, the bridge is a photographer's dream and a beautiful reminder of the craftsmanship that shaped early American highways.

Whether you love architecture, history, or simply quiet moments on the road, the Rainbow Bridge is a must-see stop that captures the timeless charm of Route 66.

46. Baxter Springs Heritage Center & Museum, Baxter Springs

This impressive museum offers a deep dive into the history of Baxter Springs, from its early settlers and Civil War significance to its golden age along Route 66. The building is fully accessible, with wide pathways and thoughtfully designed exhibits.

Inside, you'll find Civil War artifacts, pioneer history, Route 66 memorabilia, and interactive displays for all ages!

The friendly staff brings the stories to life, making this museum a standout stop for travelers who want to understand the human side of the Mother Road. After exploring, take a stroll through Baxter Springs' charming downtown, where history and hospitality blend seamlessly.

47. Luigi's Pit Stop, Galena

Luigi's Pit Stop is a playful, colorful tribute to Pixar's *Cars*, complete with interactive murals and classic cars that bring the movie's characters to life. The star is **Luigi**, a bright yellow 1959 Fiat 500 bursting out of a 3D mural, perfect for photos.

You'll also find a 1949 Mercury police car as Sheriff, a nod to Lightning McQueen, murals celebrating Route 66, Kansas, and *The Wizard of Oz.*

It's cheerful, whimsical, and guaranteed to add a little movie magic to your Route 66 adventure.

Swimming with penguins at Tanganyika Wildlife Park, Goddard KS

Bonus Side Quest: Swim with Penguins in Kansas!

If you're up for a detour, head to **Tanganyika Wildlife Park in Goddard, Kansas,** the *only* place in the United States where you can **swim with penguins**. It's an unforgettable experience and a fun addition to any Kansas itinerary.

There's a moment, just south of Baxter Springs, where Kansas begins to fade behind you, and Oklahoma appears ahead, not with fanfare, but with a quiet widening of the world. The sky stretches a little farther. The horizon pulls back. The road straightens into something long and steady, like a deep breath you didn't realize you were holding.

Kansas was small but powerful, a reminder that meaning doesn't need miles to matter. It gave you intimacy, connection, and the kind of gentle moments that settle into your memory long after the journey ends. Kansas taught you to slow down. To notice. To listen. To trust the road and yourself.

Crossing into Oklahoma feels like stepping into a new chapter of confidence.

The landscape opens. The air shifts. The road begins to hum with possibility.

It's as if the Mother Road is saying, *"You've found your rhythm. Now let's see where it can take you."*

This border carries its own kind of symbolism. Kansas is where you learned what works, the pacing, the packing, the pauses, the ways your family moves together. Oklahoma is where you begin to feel steady. Capable. Ready for the long stretch ahead.

There's a quiet pride in that.

As you cross the state line, you feel the road expand beneath you. The kids lean forward, curious about what's next. Elijah's siblings point out the change in scenery. And you, you feel something settle inside you. A sense of belonging. A sense of momentum. A sense that you're not just traveling Route 66 anymore.

You're becoming part of it.

The miles ahead are long, but they're full of heart. And Oklahoma is ready to welcome you with open sky and open arms.

Capture Your Favorite Moments in Kansas

Memory	Route 66 Location	What Happened	Who You Were With	Why It Stuck With You
1				
2				
3				
4				
5				

Kansas Reflection Questions

The Shortest Stretch with the Biggest Heart

- What does Kansas's short but meaningful stretch of Route 66 say about the value of "small" moments?
- How did Kansas remind you that even brief stops can hold deep significance?
- What did Kansas teach you about the resilience of small communities along the Mother Road?
- What conversations or encounters reminded you of the human side of Route 66?
- Did the slower, quieter pace of this stretch change how you experienced the journey?

4

Oklahoma

HEARTLAND CONNECTION

Open roads and open sky.

Oklahoma holds the **longest drivable stretch of Route 66,** more than 400 miles of open sky, rolling plains, small towns, and big stories. This is where the road feels endless in the best possible way. Where the horizon becomes a companion. Where the miles begin to soften you, steady you, and remind you that travel isn't just about movement, it's about meaning.

For families, Oklahoma is a playground of quirky roadside icons, hands-on museums, and wide-open spaces. For accessibility-minded travelers, it's a place where thoughtful design meets genuine hospitality. And for anyone carrying a story, a hope, a worry, a child, a dream, Oklahoma offers room to breathe.

Giant Neon Soda at Pops 66 Soda Ranch

48. Pops 66 Soda Ranch, Arcadia

There's something joyful about walking into a place lined floor-to-ceiling with soda bottles arranged by color, a rainbow of fizz and nostalgia. **Pops 66 Soda Ranch** is part diner, part gas station, part roadside wonder, and entirely delightful.

Kids run from shelf to shelf, pointing out flavors they've never heard of. Adults smile at the classics from their childhood. And everyone stops to admire the towering neon soda bottle outside, glowing like a beacon at night.

The wide pathways, level entrances, and open layout make it easy for everyone to explore. Whether you're sipping a quirky soda or snapping photos under the neon glow, Pops is a reminder that joy often comes in bright, bubbly moments.

49. Gateway to Route 66, Miami

The town of **Miami** (pronounced "My-am-uh") is the first major stop after leaving Kansas, and it greets travelers with a grand archway that feels like a warm handshake from the Mother Road.

The longest Main Street on Route 66 runs right through town, lined with history, charm, and a sense of pride that's impossible to miss. The accessible sidewalks and friendly locals make it easy to explore.

It's a place that whispers, *You're really doing this. Keep going.*

50. Coleman Theater, Miami

Stepping into the **Coleman Theater** feels like stepping into a dream stitched in velvet and gold. Built in 1929, this Spanish Mission-style gem is filled with ornate details, sweeping staircases, and a sense of old-Hollywood glamour.

The theater is thoughtfully accessible, with staff who go out of their way to welcome every visitor. Whether you're attending a show or taking a guided tour, the Coleman wraps you in wonder, a reminder that beauty and history can coexist in the most unexpected places.

51. Afton Station Packard Museum, Afton

This cozy museum, housed in a restored 1930s filling station, feels like a love letter to the golden age of American motoring. Classic Packards gleam under the lights, each one telling a story of craftsmanship and adventure.

The layout is accessible and easy to navigate, and the staff is warm, knowledgeable, and eager to share the history of the cars and the town.

It's a small stop with a big heart, the kind that stays with you long after you leave.

52. Blue Whale, Catoosa

Few Route 66 icons are as beloved, or as delightfully odd, as the **Blue Whale**. This cheerful, bright-blue giant sits beside a peaceful pond, inviting travelers to wander, rest, and smile.

The surrounding park is accessible, with level pathways and shaded picnic areas. Kids love exploring the whale's friendly grin. Adults love the nostalgia. And everyone leaves with a photo and a memory.

It's quick. It's quirky. It's pure Route 66 magic.

53. Will Rogers Memorial Museum, Claremore

Perched on a hill overlooking Claremore, the **Will Rogers Memorial Museum** celebrates the life of America's cowboy-philosopher, a man whose humor, wisdom, and humanity still resonate today.

The museum is spacious, accessible, and filled with interactive exhibits, film clips, and memorabilia. The views from the grounds are breathtaking, and the atmosphere feels peaceful and reflective.

It's a place that reminds you of the power of kindness, humor, and storytelling values that echo through the Mother Road.

54. Totem Pole Park, Foyil

Created by folk artist Ed Galloway, **Totem Pole Park** is a whimsical outdoor wonderland bursting with color and creativity. The towering concrete totem pole, the largest in the world, rises from the Oklahoma landscape like something out of a storybook.

Accessible pathways wind through the park, inviting visitors to explore the sculptures up close. It's playful, imaginative, and deeply human, a reminder that art doesn't have to be perfect to be meaningful.

55. Tulsa Route 66 Historical Village, Tulsa

This open-air museum brings Tulsa's early-day boom to life with restored structures, replicas, and a towering oil derrick that nods to the city's past.

Wide walkways and open spaces make it easy for families and mobility-device users to explore. Interpretive signs share stories of Tulsa's role along the Mother Road.

It's a cheerful, educational stop that blends history with hands-on fun.

Center of the Universe, Tulsa

56. Center of the Universe, Tulsa

One of the quirkiest stops on Route 66, the **Center of the Universe** is a small concrete circle with a big secret: when you stand inside it and speak, your voice echoes back louder and distorted, but only to you.

The kids love shouting silly phrases! The surrounding plaza is accessible and easy to navigate. It's a quick stop, but one that leaves you smiling.

57. Oklahoma Route 66 Museum, Clinton

This vibrant museum takes you through every era of Route 66, from Dust Bowl migration to neon-lit diners. Interactive exhibits, vintage cars, recreated scenes, and nostalgic music make it a lively, immersive experience.

The layout is fully accessible, with wide pathways and clear signage. It's a must-see stop for anyone who wants to understand the heart of the Mother Road.

58. The Threatt Filling Station, Luther

Just outside Oklahoma City sits the historic **Threatt Filling Station**, one of the few Black-owned businesses on Route 66 during the Jim Crow era. For Black travelers, it was a rare place of safety a stop where families could rest, refuel, and breathe without fear.

Today, the weathered building stands as a powerful reminder that travel hasn't always been equal. For families navigating disability, the Threatt Station echoes a familiar truth: accessible travel begins with dignity and the right to feel safe on the road.

Even in restoration, it remains a landmark of resilience a place worth pausing to honor the generations who made the Mother Road safer for those who came after them.

59. Elk City Route 66 Museum Complex, Elk City

This multi-building complex is a joyful deep dive into Route 66 history. Recreated streetscapes, vintage vehicles, themed galleries, and immersive exhibits make it feel like a mini-town dedicated to the Mother Road.

Accessible walkways, ramps, and spacious galleries ensure everyone can explore comfortably.

It's colorful, nostalgic, and full of surprises.

Strafford Air &Space Museum

60. Stafford Air & Space Museum, Weatherford

A breathtaking tribute to aviation and space exploration, this museum honors astronaut Thomas P. Stafford with real spacecraft, historic aircraft, and hands-on exhibits.

Wide pathways, ramps, and accessible displays make it easy for all visitors to enjoy. Kids marvel at the rockets. Adults linger over the engineering. Grandparents often share stories of the space race.

It's inspiring, a reminder that exploration takes courage, curiosity, and heart.

Oklahoma leaves you with a sense of steadiness, the kind that comes from long miles, open skies, and the quiet confidence of knowing you've found your rhythm. It's the state where you learned to trust the road, trust your pace, and trust your family's way of traveling. It's where the journey stopped feeling new and started feeling natural.

The sky somehow gets bigger. The colors sharpen. The wind picks up, carrying dust and sunlight and a little bit of swagger.

It's as if the Mother Road is nudging you, saying, *"You've found your footing. Now let's have some fun."*

For families traveling with accessibility needs, this border carries its own kind of courage. Oklahoma taught you endurance, the long stretch, the pacing, the patience with all the "Are we there yet?". Texas invites you to embrace boldness. To lean into joy. To let the road surprise you again.

There's a spark in that.

As we cross the state line, the kids point out the change in landscape, the flatness, the openness, the way the horizon seems to stretch into forever. I feel the shift, too. A sense of possibility. A sense of play. A sense that the road is about to show me something unforgettable.

Texas doesn't whisper. She arrives with neon, nostalgia, and a grin.

And as the first miles unfold beneath your wheels, you realize that this border isn't just a transition, it's an invitation. To be bold. To be curious. To let the journey expand you in ways you didn't expect.

The road ahead is bright, loud, and full of heart.

Capture Your Favorite Moments in Oklahoma

Memory	Route 66 Location	What Happened	Who You Were With	Why It Stuck With You
1				
2				
3				
4				
5				

Oklahoma Reflection Questions

Heartland Connection

- What moment in Oklahoma made you feel connected to the road, to your family, or to yourself?
- How did the wide-open landscapes shape your experience of the journey?
- Which quirky roadside stop made you smile the most?
- What stories or conversations from this stretch will you carry forward?
- How did Oklahoma remind you of resilience, reinvention, or hope?

5

———————————

Texas

BOLDNESS & CONTRAST

Where the sky gets bigger, the stories get louder

Crossing into Texas on Route 66 feels like stepping into a widescreen movie, the kind where the horizon goes on forever, and the landscape shifts from quiet plains to neon-lit diners without warning. Texas may only hold about 150 drivable miles of the Mother Road, but every inch of it is packed with character. This is a place where the road feels both intimate and enormous, where the smallest towns hold the biggest stories, and where the journey becomes a little bolder, a little braver, and a lot more fun.

Texas is a contrast. It's wide-open silence and over-the-top spectacle. It's ghost towns and giant crosses, retro diners and modern art installations. It's the kind of place that reminds you that adventure doesn't have to be complicated, it just has to be lived.

Cadillac Ranch Amarillo TX

61. Tower Station & U-Drop Inn Café, Shamrock

The **U-Drop Inn** rises from the Texas plains like a neon-tipped time capsule, all Art Deco angles, gleaming tilework, and retro charm. Built in 1936, it's one of the most photographed stops on Route 66, and for good reason. When the sun hits the green and cream façade, it feels like the building itself is glowing.

Inside, the restored café and visitor center offer a warm, nostalgic atmosphere. Families linger over snacks, kids marvel at the vintage décor, and adults soak in the history. The accessible pathways, level entrances, and friendly staff make it easy for everyone to explore.

At night, when the neon flickers to life, the whole building becomes a beacon, a reminder that beauty can bloom even in the quietest corners of the world.

62. Devil's Rope Museum, McLean

Only on Route 66 could a museum dedicated to **barbed wire** become a must-see attraction, and yet the **Devil's Rope Museum** is unexpectedly fascinating. Rows of barbed-wire varieties, vintage ranching tools, and quirky art pieces tell the story of how a simple invention shaped the American West.

Kids get wide-eyed. Grandparents get nostalgic. Adults find themselves saying, "I had no idea this could be so interesting."

The museum is spacious, accessible, and filled with friendly volunteers who love sharing stories. It's a stop that reminds you that history is often hiding in the most ordinary things, waiting for someone curious enough to look closer.

Giant Groom Cross, Groom, TX

63. The Groom Cross, Groom

You see it long before you arrive, a gleaming steel cross rising 190 feet into the Texas sky. The **Groom Cross** is one of those landmarks that makes you instinctively quiet, not out of reverence alone, but because the sheer scale of it takes your breath away.

Accessible pathways wind through the surrounding sculptures, each one telling a story. Benches offer places to rest and reflect. The air feels still here, even when the wind moves across the plains.

It's a peaceful stop, grounding, humbling, and unexpectedly moving.

64. Old-Fashioned Cherry Limeade at the Pharmacy, Panhandle

Some memories taste like childhood. For me, this one *is* childhood. It is a little off Route 66, but this is the town I grew up in, and we always stop here for a stroll down memory lane.

The small-town pharmacy in Panhandle, Texas, still serves cherry limeades the old-fashioned way, in real glasses, with bright syrup, fresh-squeezed lime, and that perfect fizzy sparkle. Kids love the sweetness. Adults love the nostalgia. Grandparents often share stories of their own soda-fountain afternoons.

The level entrance, wide aisles, and friendly staff make it easy for everyone to enjoy. It's a simple stop, but one that fills your heart, a reminder that joy often hides in the familiar.

65. The Big Texan Steak Ranch, Amarillo

Bold, loud, neon-soaked, and unapologetically Texan, the **Big Texan Steak Ranch** is a spectacle in the best possible way. Giant billboards, taxidermy, themed dining rooms, and the famous **72-ounce steak challenge** make it one of the most iconic stops on Route 66.

Kids love the shooting gallery. Adults love the hearty meals. Everyone loves the energy.

Accessible entrances, wide walkways, and spacious seating make it easy for families and mobility-device users to enjoy. It's a place where laughter comes easily, and memories come quickly.

66. Cadillac Ranch, Amarillo

Few Route 66 stops capture the spirit of creativity and rebellion like **Cadillac Ranch,** ten vintage Cadillacs buried nose-down in the Texas earth, each one layered with decades of spray-painted color.

It's art. It's chaos. It's joy. My mini-humans love it!

Families bring cans of paint and leave their mark. Teens pose for photos. Adults marvel at the ever-changing canvas. The open layout makes it easy to explore, though the ground can be uneven after rain.

It's a stop that reminds you that art doesn't have to be quiet, sometimes it's loud, messy, and wonderfully alive.

Midway, Adrian, TX

67. Midpoint Café, Adrian

Welcome to the exact halfway point of Route 66. It is **1,139 miles from Chicago and 1,139 miles from Santa Monica**. The **Midpoint Café** is pure Americana charm, famous for its "ugly crust" pies and warm, small-town hospitality.

Travelers from around the world gather here, swapping stories, snapping photos, and celebrating the moment they've reached the middle of the Mother Road.

The café is accessible, cozy, and full of heart, a reminder that the journey is just as important as the destination.

68. Dream Maker Garage, Adrian

Just steps from the midpoint sign, the **Dream Maker Garage** feels like stepping into a living postcard. Restored service-station vibes, quirky décor, local art, and a famously friendly cat make this stop unforgettable.

The owners, Kelly and Jason, welcome travelers like old friends. Their gift shop is filled with Route 66 treasures, and their Airbnb cabins offer a chance to sleep right in the heart of the Mother Road.

Accessible pathways and a relaxed atmosphere make it easy for everyone to enjoy. It's a stop that feels like home, even if you've never been there before.

69. Glenrio Historic District, Glenrio

Straddling the Texas–New Mexico border, **Glenrio** is a ghost town frozen in time. Abandoned motels, empty storefronts, and weathered signs whisper stories of travelers who once filled the streets.

There is an eerie quiet that the kids love. Standing here, you feel the weight of the history of a time when Glenrio was still alive with neon and traffic.

The wide, level dirt paths make it easy to explore. It's a place that invites reflection, a reminder that even the busiest roads can fall silent, but their stories remain.

Boldness leaves its mark *as* you prepare to leave Texas, you realize how much this stretch has expanded you. The neon nights. The wide-open mornings. The art installations rising from the earth like secrets. The diners where strangers became friends. The moments of pure, unfiltered joy that surprised you when you needed them most.

Texas is loud in all the right ways. She reminds you that joy can be big. That memories can be messy and colorful. That adventure can be bold and still be accessible.

For families like ours, Texas offers something rare, permission to embrace the fun without apology. To let the kids spray paint a Cadillac. To laugh at the over-the-top steakhouse signs. To celebrate reaching the midpoint of the Mother Road.

Texas teaches you that accessibility isn't just about ramps and restrooms. It's about belonging. It's about being welcomed into the story fully, joyfully, loudly.

As the state line approaches, you feel a spark of gratitude. For the boldness. For the beauty. For the reminder that your family deserves joy that takes up space.

Texas doesn't just move you west. She moves you forward.

Capture Your Favorite Moments in Texas

Memory	Route 66 Location	What Happened	Who You Were With	Why It Stuck With You
1				
2				
3				
4				
5				

Texas Reflection Questions

Boldness & Contrast

- Which Texas landmark surprised you the most and why?
- How did the wide-open skies and long horizons shape your experience?
- What small-town moment reminded you of the heart of Route 66?
- Which quirky stop made you laugh, pause, or reflect?
- How did Texas invite you to embrace boldness, joy, or curiosity?

6

New Mexico

COLOR, CULTURE & SPIRITUAL QUIET

Where the desert breathes, the colors deepen, and the Mother Road invites you inward.

Crossing into New Mexico feels like entering a painting, adobe towns glowing in the sun, neon signs flickering awake at dusk, and desert horizons stretching toward distant mountains. The air feels different here. Softer. Older. As if the land itself remembers every traveler who has ever passed through.

New Mexico has 535 miles of Route 66, one of the longest and richest stretches of the highway. And unlike any other state, Route 66 was realigned here *twice*, giving it three distinct historic paths. More routes mean more stories. More cultures. More layers. More opportunities to be changed by the road.

This is where the journey slows down. Where the colors shift from gold to red to violet. Where the sky feels impossibly wide. Where the road becomes not just a path, but a teacher.

Continental Divide on Route 66 Exit 47

70. Route 66 Diner, Gallup

There's something comforting about a diner, the clink of silverware, the hum of conversation, the smell of something warm and familiar. The **Route 66 Diner in Gallup** captures that feeling perfectly.

Chrome accents. Cozy booths. A menu that blends American classics with New Mexico favorites. And the Navajo tacos? They're the kind of meal that becomes a memory.

My kids love the milkshakes and the green-chile dishes. It is a place where everyone feels welcome.

The level entrances, wide pathways, and attentive staff make it easy for all travelers to enjoy. It's a place where the road slows down, where you can breathe, laugh, and feel the warmth of small-town hospitality.

71. Mesalands Dinosaur Museum, Tucumcari

If you want to watch a child's imagination ignite, bring them to the **Mesalands Dinosaur Museum**. Towering skeletons, bronze sculptures, and real fossils make the museum feel alive with ancient stories.

One of my favorite things here is the massive Torvosaurus.

Wide walkways, spacious galleries, and well-lit displays make it accessible and comfortable for all. It's a stop that reminds you that the land beneath Route 66 holds stories millions of years older than the highway itself.

72. Route 66 Auto Museum, Santa Rosa

Chrome. Neon. Nostalgia. The **Route 66 Auto Museum** is a love letter to America's romance with the open road. More than 30 restored classics shine under the lights, each one telling a story of freedom, craftsmanship, and adventure.

Kids point out their favorites. Adults reminisce. Grandparents smile at memories of cars they once drove.

The museum is fully accessible, with wide walkways and friendly staff. It's a joyful stop, one that celebrates the heart of Route 66.

73. San Miguel Chapel, Santa Fe

Stepping into **San Miguel Chapel** feels like stepping into a whispered prayer. Often called the oldest church in the United States, this humble adobe sanctuary has stood since around 1610.

The thick walls hold a cool, peaceful stillness. The carved altar glows softly. The air feels sacred, no matter your beliefs.

It's a place to pause, breathe, and remember that the journey is not just about movement, it's about meaning.

74. Blue Hole, Santa Rosa

In the middle of the desert, the **Blue Hole** appears like a miracle, a sapphire-blue artesian spring plunging more than 80 feet deep.

Even from a seated position behind the stone wall, the water's clarity and color are mesmerizing. Divers slip beneath the surface. Families gather for photos. Travelers pause to cool off and marvel at this unexpected oasis.

The paths are accessible, even if the water itself is not. And the moment, the stillness, the color, the surprise, is unforgettable.

75. Loretto Chapel, Santa Fe

The **Loretto Chapel** feels like a fairy tale tucked into the heart of Santa Fe. Built in the 1870s, this Gothic-Revival gem is famous for its "Miraculous Staircase," a graceful wooden spiral with no visible means of support.

Our family loves the sense of wonder the staircase inspires, the kids get captivated by the mystery behind its construction, and appreciate the craftsmanship and peaceful atmosphere. It's a serene, beautiful place to pause, reflect, and soak in Santa Fe's rich spiritual and artistic heritage.

The stained-glass windows cast soft colors across the pews, and the quiet inside feels sacred. It's a peaceful, inspiring stop, a reminder that wonder still exists in the world.

76. Sandia Peak Tramway, Albuquerque

Riding the **Sandia Peak Tramway** feels like lifting off into another world. One of the most breathtaking experiences along New Mexico's stretch of Route 66, the Sandia Peak Tramway carries visitors high above the desert floor to the crest of the Sandia Mountains. As the longest aerial tramway in North America, it offers sweeping views of deep canyons, rugged cliffs, and the vast Rio Grande Valley.

The kids press their faces to the glass, fall silent as the Rio Grande Valley unfolds beneath them. We breathe in the cool mountain air at the summit. It is truly unforgettable.

The tramway is fully accessible, with level boarding, wide viewing areas, and attentive staff. It's a moment of awe, a reminder that beauty can be both vast and intimate.

77. Rex Museum, Gallup

The Rex Museum sits inside a sandstone building that has lived many lives. It offers a fascinating look into Gallup's layered past, from its railroad roots and mining history to its vibrant Native American and Southwestern cultural heritage. Once a hotel, brothel, billiard hall, and even a bowling alley, the building itself tells a story before you even step inside.

Inside, photographs, artifacts, and local memorabilia paint a vivid picture of a town shaped by railroads, mining, and cultural heritage.

The museum is easy to navigate, with ground-level entry and open interior spaces. It's a quiet, meaningful stop that honors the people who built this corner of the Mother Road.

78. Route 66 Neon Drive-Thru Sign, Grants

Few Route 66 stops capture pure joy like the **Neon Drive-Thru Sign** in Grants. It is one of the most photogenic stops in western New Mexico, is a glowing tribute to the Mother Road's electric personality. Shaped like a giant neon archway, this vibrant landmark invites travelers to literally *drive through Route 66 history*. Its bold colors and retro styling make it a favorite for family photos, road-trip selfies, and nighttime visits when the sign shines brightest against the desert sky.

At night, the neon shines against the desert sky. The kids love the novelty of driving under a neon sign. It's a quick, joyful stop that captures the playful spirit of Route 66 in a single glowing frame.

It's accessible whether you stay in your vehicle or explore on foot. A quick stop, but one that leaves a bright, happy memory.

79. The Singing Road, Tijeras

Some Route 66 moments are big. Others are small and surprising, like the **Singing Road** in Tijeras.One of the most delightfully quirky attractions along New Mexico's stretch of Route 66, the "Singing Road" . It turns an ordinary drive into a musical moment.

When your tires line up with a special rumble strip at exactly 45 mph, the pavement plays a portion of "America the Beautiful."

Originally created in 2014 as part of a National Geographic project, the musical rumble strip sits along NM 333 (historic Route 66) between mile markers 4 and 5. Even though official signage has come and gone over the years, the melody still plays, and travelers continue to seek it out for that magical moment when the road itself starts to sing.

The best part? It's fully accessible because the experience takes place entirely inside your vehicle.

It's a simple, joyful moment, one that literally puts music beneath your wheels.

The quiet moments stay with you the longest. As you prepare to leave New Mexico, you realize how deeply this stretch has settled into your heart. The soft glow of adobe at sunset. The hum of the Sandia Tramway rising into the sky. The laughter echoing through the Route 66 Diner. The quiet reverence inside Loretto Chapel. The desert wind brushing against your skin like a whispered reminder to slow down.

New Mexico doesn't shout. She sings.

She teaches you that beauty doesn't need to be loud to be powerful. That rest is not a pause in the journey it's part of the journey. That your family deserves moments of stillness just as much as moments of excitement.

For families traveling with medically complex children, New Mexico offers something rare space. Space to breathe. Space to adjust. Space to simply be. The kind of space that holds you gently and reminds you that you're doing better than you think.

As the state line approaches, you feel a quiet gratitude. For the colors. For the culture. For the calm. For the way this chapter softened you in all the right places.

New Mexico doesn't just move you west. She moves you inward.

Capture Your Favorite Moments in New Mexico

Memory	Route 66 Location	What Happened	Who You Were With	Why It Stuck With You
1				
2				
3				
4				
5				

New Mexico Reflection Questions

Color, Culture & Spiritual Quiet

- How did New Mexico's blend of cultures shape your experience?
- What colors, landscapes, or moments felt grounding or peaceful?
- How did this stretch of the Mother Road invite you to slow down and be present?
- Did any moment here feel spiritual, quiet, or unexpectedly meaningful?
- What conversations, meals, or encounters stayed with you long after you left?

7

Arizona

AWE, REFLECTION & GROUNDING

Where the road invites you to slow down and listen.

Crossing into Arizona feels like entering a different world, one shaped by wind, stone, and time itself. The land here is old in a way you can feel in your bones. Red-rock mesas rise like monuments. Painted deserts ripple with color. The sky stretches so wide it feels like it could swallow every worry you brought with you.

Arizona holds the **longest uninterrupted stretch of Route 66.** There are 385 miles of wide-open desert, mountain towns, neon nostalgia, and natural wonders that feel almost otherworldly. This is where the journey becomes quieter, deeper, more reflective. Where the road stops being just a road and becomes a teacher.

Grand Canyon South Rim

80. Petrified Forest National Park, Holbrook

There are places that make you feel small in the best possible way, places that remind you how ancient the world is and how lucky we are to witness it. **Petrified Forest National Park** is one of those places. It offers a landscape unlike anywhere else in the world. Here, ancient trees turned to stone lie scattered across colorful badlands, creating a surreal blend of geology, history, and desert beauty.

Here, the otherworldly feel of the terrain, 200-million-year-old trees turned to stone, lie scattered across rainbow-striped badlands. The landscape feels like a dream, quiet, surreal, humbling.

Accessible trails like **Crystal Forest**, **Giant Logs**, and **Puerco Pueblo** offer smooth, level paths with breathtaking views. Overlooks provide sweeping panoramas without long walks. Visitor centers offer accessible exhibits, restrooms, and staff who greet you with warmth.

Kids marvel at the massive petrified logs. We fall silent at the Painted Desert. With a whisper, "I've never seen anything like this."

It's a place that grounds you, a reminder that the world is ancient, resilient, and full of wonder.

Meteor Crater, Winslow, AZ

81. Meteor Crater, Winslow

Standing at the rim of **Meteor Crater** feels like staring into the Earth's memory. It offers a jaw-dropping look at the power of the cosmos. Formed about 50,000 years ago when a massive iron-nickel meteorite slammed into the Earth, this enormous bowl stretches nearly a mile across and plunges more than 550 feet deep.

This is one of our favorite awe-inspiring stops along the way! It is a stop that brings Earth's cosmic past to life.

Accessible viewing platforms offer stunning, unobstructed views without steep climbs. The visitor center is fully accessible, with ramps, elevators, exhibits, and theaters designed for all abilities.

It's a stop that reminds you of the power of the universe, and the fragility of our tiny place within it.

82. Standin' on the Corner Park, Winslow

A small corner in a small town, but one that carries a big piece of American music history. Inspired by the Eagles' "Take It Easy," **Standin' on the Corner Park** invites travelers to step into the song. The park blends nostalgia, music history, and small-town charm, making it a fun and memorable stop.

The brick plaza is smooth and accessible. The bronze statue holds a guitar. The mural behind him sets the scene. And the vibe? Pure Route 66 joy.

It's a quick stop, but one that fills your heart.

83. La Posada Hotel, Winslow

If Route 66 has a crown jewel, **La Posada Hotel** might be it. Designed in 1929 by famed architect Mary Colter for the Fred Harvey Company, this beautifully restored hotel blends Spanish Colonial Revival architecture with lush gardens, handcrafted details, and a timeless elegance that transports visitors to another era.

Sunlit hallways. Hand-carved details. Lush gardens. Original artwork. A sense of timeless beauty.

Accessible rooms, level pathways, wide hallways, and attentive staff make it a welcoming stay for all travelers. Explore the gardens, savor the Turquoise Room's cuisine, and explore the golden age of rail travel. It served as a grand stop for Santa Fe Railway passengers.

It's a place that invites you to slow down, breathe deeply, and savor the moment.

84. Lowell Observatory, Flagstaff

Perched high in the pines of Flagstaff, **Lowell Observatory** is where Pluto was discovered, and where countless visitors have fallen in love with the night sky.

Day or night, the observatory offers something magical. Solar viewing sessions. Historic telescope tours. Interactive science exhibits. Evening stargazing programs

Accessible pathways, ramps, telescope stations, and helpful staff ensure that everyone can participate in the wonder.

It's a stop that reminds you how vast and beautiful the universe truly is.

85. Walnut Canyon National Monument, Flagstaff

Walnut Canyon is a place where history clings to the cliffs. More than 700 years ago, the Sinagua people built homes in the canyon walls that still stand today, sheltered by stone and time.

The accessible **Rim Trail** offers paved, level pathways with breathtaking views of the canyon and its ancient homes. Benches and shaded areas invite you to rest, reflect, and imagine the lives once lived here.

It's a stop that connects you to the past and to the resilience of the human spirit.

86. Grand Canyon Caverns, Peach Springs

Descending into the **Grand Canyon Caverns** feels like entering the Earth's quiet heart. These dry caverns, among the largest in the U.S., sit 200–300 feet below the surface, cool, still, and awe-inspiring.

An elevator takes visitors directly to the main cavern level, eliminating the need for stairs. Wide walkways, handrails, and attentive guides make the experience accessible and comfortable.

We love the echoing chambers, the formations, and the history. Including the caverns' role as a Cold War fallout shelter.

It's a stop that feels both adventurous and peaceful.

Bearizona Williams

87. Bearizona, Williams

Part wildlife safari, part walk-through zoo, Bearizona blends the excitement of a safari with the charm of a walk-through zoo, all set amid the tall pines of northern Arizona. This family-friendly wildlife park lets visitors experience North American animals up close, from the comfort of their own vehicle or along beautifully designed walking paths.

The drive-through portion lets you see bison, wolves, burros, and, of course, bears from the comfort of your vehicle. The walk-through area offers shaded paths, animal shows, and interactive exhibits.

Accessible parking, restrooms, pathways, and viewing areas make it easy for everyone to enjoy.

It's a stop that fills your heart with wonder.

Oatman Ghost Town

88. Oatman Ghost Town, Oatman

If Route 66 had a wild west heartbeat, it would be **Oatman**. With its wonderfully eccentric stop along the western edge of Route 66, Oatman Ghost Town feels like stepping straight into an Old West movie, only with far more burros. Once a booming gold-mining town, Oatman now thrives as a lively, character-filled destination where wooden boardwalks, rustic storefronts, and staged gunfights bring history to life. The real stars, of course, are the wild burros that wander freely through town, greeting visitors with gentle curiosity and plenty of photo opportunities.

You will adore feeding the burros, the quirky shops, and the old-west charm.

The main street is level and walkable/rollable, with accessible parking nearby. Shaded seating areas offer places to rest and watch the burros wander by.

It's chaotic, charming, and unforgettable.

89. Route 66 Museum, Kingman

Inside the historic Powerhouse Building, the **Route 66 Museum** in Kingman brings the Mother Road's history to life with immersive exhibits, vintage vehicles, and recreated scenes.

Visitors of all ages love the life-size dioramas, vintage vehicles, and evocative displays that recreate the sights, sounds, and stories of travelers who shaped the highway's legacy. Accessible pathways, elevators, and well-lit displays make it easy for everyone to explore.

You can find a classic car, step into a recreated 1910s tent camp, or learning about Dust Bowl migrants. The Route 66 Museum in Kingman offers an accessible, engaging journey through the heart and history of Route 66. It's a stop that honors the generations who traveled this road before us.

90. Hackberry General Store, Hackberry

Hackberry General Store is pure nostalgia wrapped in weathered wood, vintage signs, and classic Americana charm. Often called a "living postcard," this quirky stop feels like stepping into a time capsule of the Mother Road's golden era. The exterior, with its old gas pumps, rusted cars, and neon signs, is a photographer's dream, while the inside overflows with Route 66 memorabilia, souvenirs, and historic curiosities.

Accessible outdoor areas, level ground, and wide doorways make it easy to explore.

It's another stop that feels like stepping into a living postcard.

91. Roadkill Café, Seligman

Don't worry, the menu is all jokes. But the food? Delicious. It is famous for its playful, tongue-in-cheek "roadkill-themed" menu, with dishes named *"Splatter Platter"* or *"Dead Meat Treat."* Don't worry, though: the food is delicious, freshly prepared, and entirely free of actual roadkill. The café leans into the joke with gusto, creating a fun, lighthearted atmosphere that travelers of all ages enjoy.

The **Roadkill Café** leans into Route 66 humor with playful menu names and rustic décor. Accessible entrances, spacious seating, and friendly staff make it a welcoming stop for all.

It's silly, warm, and wonderfully Route 66.

92. Jack Rabbit Trading Post, Joseph City

"HERE IT IS."

The famous billboard leads you to the **Jack Rabbit Trading Post**, a classic curio shop filled with Route 66 souvenirs, vintage memorabilia, and friendly conversation.

Accessible parking, level ground, and wide entrances make it easy to explore.

We love the giant jackrabbit statue. Inside, the shop is packed with Route 66 souvenirs, vintage memorabilia, local crafts, and friendly conversation from the long-time owners. Outside, the old gas pumps, weathered signage, and desert backdrop make it a perfect photo stop.

It's a stop that captures the playful spirit of the Mother Road.

Bonus Side Quests:

If you want to take a side quest, you can spend a couple of days at the Grand Canyon, it is about an hour from Williams, or drive up from Kingman and spend the day touring Hoover Dam. Both of these detours feel like bonus levels on a Route 66 adventure, and they're absolutely worth the time.

Williams is one of the most convenient jumping-off points for the South Rim. It's roughly an hour's drive, and the route is smooth, scenic, and easy to navigate. Spending a couple of days at the canyon gives you time to. Explore multiple overlooks along Desert View Drive. Catch sunrise or sunset (both are unforgettable). Visit the accessible Rim Trail, which offers miles of paved trail with breathtaking views. Enjoy ranger programs, visitor centers, and the historic El Tovar area

If you want to make it even more fun, the Grand Canyon Railway departs right from Williams and takes you straight to the South Rim, a great option for families or anyone who prefers to skip the drive.

From Kingman, the Hoover Dam is an easy and rewarding day trip. The drive is about 75 minutes, and the dam itself is a marvel of engineering and history. Once there, you can. Walk across the top of the dam. Explore the visitor center and exhibits. Take a guided tour inside the dam (with accessible options). Enjoy sweeping views from the Mike O'Callaghan–Pat Tillman Memorial Bridge. It's one of those places where the scale hits you the moment you step out of the car.

Both destinations blend seamlessly into a Route 66 itinerary because they expand the story of the American West's natural wonders on one side and human ingenuity on the other.

Some landscapes stay with you forever. As you prepare to leave Arizona, you realize how deeply this stretch has imprinted itself on your memory. The painted hills. The petrified logs glowing in the sun. The quiet power of Meteor Crater. The nostalgia of Seligman. The winding roads through Oatman where burros wander like they own the place.

Arizona is a chapter of contrasts rugged and tender, ancient and playful, vast and intimate all at once. She reminds you that the world is bigger than your worries, older than your fears, and more beautiful than you remembered.

For families traveling with medically complex children, Arizona offers something rare awe. The kind that lifts you out of the daily grind and reminds you that your family deserves moments of wonder. The kind that makes the hard days feel lighter. The kind that stays with you long after the journey ends.

As the state line approaches, you feel a quiet gratitude. For the colors. For the canyons. For the laughter echoing through small desert towns. For the reminder that beauty can be both wild and welcoming.

Arizona doesn't just move you west. She moves you beyond yourself.

Capture Your Favorite Moments in Arizona

Memory	Route 66 Location	What Happened	Who You Were With	Why It Stuck With You
1				
2				
3				
4				
5				

Arizona Reflection Questions

Awe, Reflection & Grounding

- How did Arizona's vast landscapes shift your sense of time or presence?
- Which Route 66 relic stirred nostalgia or curiosity?
- Did the desert make you feel small, free, peaceful or something else entirely?
- What moment here felt grounding or spiritual?
- What conversations, meals, or encounters felt meaningful or unexpected?

8

California

ENDINGS, BEGINNINGS & TRANSFORMATION

Where the journey becomes something you carry long after the miles are behind you.

Crossing into California feels like stepping into a final chapter you've been writing toward without even realizing it. The air shifts. The light softens. The landscape transforms from desert quiet to mountain curves to palm-lined streets. California is where Route 66 ends, but it's also where something new begins.

This is the stretch where travelers reflect on the miles behind them. Where families grow closer. Where stories deepen. Where the road becomes not just a path, but a mirror.

California holds some of the most iconic Route 66 stops, neon motels, mountain towns, citrus groves, boardwalks, and finally, the Pacific Ocean. But more than that, California holds the emotional weight of the journey. It's the place where you realize how far you've come, not just in miles, but in meaning.

Cabazon Dinosaurs

92. Cabazon Dinosaurs, Cabazon

The Cabazon Dinosaurs rise out of the desert like two giant guardians of the California stretch of Route 66. Dinny the 150-foot Apatosaurus and Mr. Rex, the towering T. rex, have been delighting travelers since the 1960s, part roadside whimsy, part pop-culture icon.

Families wander the dino-themed grounds, snap photos beneath Mr. Rex's jaws, and explore the gift shop tucked inside Dinny's belly. It is not wheelchair accessible but the grounds outside are. It's pure retro magic, the kind of playful stop that reminds you why the Mother Road is unforgettable.

93. Roy's Motel & Café, Amboy

Few Route 66 landmarks are as iconic or as photogenic as **Roy's Motel & Café**. The neon sign rises from the desert like a beacon, its mid-century angles sharp against the endless sky.

The surrounding landscape is stark, silent, and breathtaking. Kids run across the gravel. Adults take photos from every angle. Grandparents remember when Roy's was buzzing with travelers.

The ground is level and easy to navigate, and the open space makes it accessible for mobility devices. It's a stop that feels like stepping into a postcard.

94. Pioneertown, Near Yucca Valley

Built in 1946 by Hollywood legends like Roy Rogers and Gene Autry, Pioneertown was designed as a fully functional Old West movie set, real buildings, real interiors, real doors swinging open into saloons and general stores.Instead of flimsy facades, the town was constructed with real wood, real doors, and real interiors so actors could film scenes outside and then walk straight into a saloon or general store for the next shot.

Today, Mane Street still feels like a frontier town paused in time. Visitors wander past stables, a jail, rustic storefronts, and artisan shops. On select weekends, mock gunfights bring the old movie magic back to life. Just steps away, Pappy & Harriet's adds live music, hearty food, and a lively desert energy.

95. Barstow Station, Barstow

Barstow Station is a classic Route 66 stop built around retired Santa Fe railcars, a playful nod to the town's railroad roots all wrapped in bright signage and Mojave Desert charm.

Inside the railcars, you'll find shops, snacks, souvenirs, and familiar fast-food options all tucked into a setting that feels like a playful nod to Barstow's deep railroad heritage. Outside, the bright signage and desert backdrop make it a fun photo stop, especially for families and Route 66 enthusiasts.

96. Route 66 Museum, Victorville

Inside the historic Powerhouse Building, the **Victorville Route 66 Museum** celebrates the Mother Road with immersive exhibits, vintage vehicles, and recreated scenes. It's packed with vintage cars, neon signs, quirky displays, and immersive exhibits that bring the highway's history to life.

Accessible pathways, ramps, and well-lit displays make it easy for everyone to enjoy. It's a stop that honors the generations who traveled this road before us and the ones who will follow.

97. Wigwam Motel, San Bernardino

A true Route 66 classic, the Wigwam Motel invites travelers to "Sleep in a Wigwam!", a slogan that has charmed road-trippers since the 1940s. Its towering concrete teepees, arranged in a semicircle beneath palm trees and neon glow, feel like stepping straight into a mid-century picture.

Inside, the rooms are cozy and updated, while still retaining their vintage charm. Even if you're not staying overnight, the Wigwam's architecture, history, and unmistakable character make it a must-see stop on the California stretch.

98. Hollywood, Los Angeles

Reaching Hollywood on your Route 66 journey feels like arriving at the heart of American storytelling. Though the Mother Road no longer officially runs through here, its spirit lives on; countless dreamers once followed Route 66 west, hoping to make it big under the California sun.

A short detour brings you to one of the most recognizable landmarks in the world, the **Hollywood Sign**, perched high in the Santa Monica Mountains like a promise written across the hillside. Seeing it up close feels different than spotting it from afar; it's bigger, bolder, and more meaningful when you're standing beneath that wide California sky.

There are several accessible viewpoints that offer stunning, crowd-free perspectives. **Lake Hollywood Park** provides a relaxed, family-friendly setting with open grassy areas perfect for photos. **Griffith Observatory** offers another iconic angle, pairing the sign with sweeping views of Los Angeles and the Pacific haze beyond.

Both locations offer smooth pathways, accessible parking, and plenty of space for wheelchairs, scooters, and strollers. The observatory includes elevators, ramps, and accessible restrooms, making it one of the most inclusive ways to experience the city's most famous view.

99. Original McDonald's Museum, San Bernardino

The Museum sits on the site of the very first **McDonald's Restaurant,** opened by the McDonald brothers in 1940. Long before the golden arches became a global symbol, this tiny hamburger stand helped pioneer the fast-food model that would change American dining forever.

Accessible entrances, wide aisles, and friendly volunteers make it easy to explore. Today, the museum is a treasure trove of nostalgia. Visitors can explore rooms filled with vintage menus, Happy Meal toys, historic uniforms, early advertising, and rare memorabilia spanning decades. The exterior features retro signage and murals that make it a fun photo stop, while inside, volunteers share stories about the McDonald brothers, the Speedee Service System, and the brand's evolution. It's quirky, colorful, and surprisingly rich in history, a perfect blend of Route 66 charm and American pop-culture heritage.

It's a fun, lighthearted stop, a reminder that even simple things can become cultural icons.

100. Santa Monica Pier, Santa Monica

This is it. The end of the road. The place where Route 66 meets the Pacific Ocean.

The **Santa Monica Pier** is vibrant, joyful, and full of life, a fitting finale to a journey that has carried you across the heart of America.

Accessible ramps, wide walkways, viewing decks, and beach wheelchairs make it possible for everyone to experience the ocean breeze, the sound of waves, and the glow of the Ferris wheel.

Kids run toward the water, breathe in the salt air, and smile at the sight of the "End of the Trail" sign.

Route 66 End of the Trail Sign Santa Monica

There's a moment, standing at the end of the Santa Monica Pier, when the world seems to pause. The waves crash beneath you. The sun glows against the horizon. The Route 66 "End of the Trail" sign stands quietly above the crowd, humble and iconic all at once.

And you feel something shift inside you.

And you, you feel everything at once.

The miles behind you. The memories you made. The challenges you overcame. The joy you allowed yourself to feel. The courage it took to begin. The strength it took to keep going.

The kids run toward the railing, pointing at the ocean with wide eyes. Elijah laughs as the wind whips through his hair. And I feel something inside me soften, a release, a relief, a gratitude so deep it almost knocks the breath from my chest.

This is not just the end of the road. It's the end of a chapter. A chapter you wrote with your family, mile by mile, moment by moment.

This moment carries a weight that only you can understand. You didn't just reach the ocean. You reached a version of yourself who believed this was possible. Who fought for it. Who made it happen.

The Mother Road doesn't ask you to be fearless. She asks you to be present. To be open. To be willing.

And as the waves crash beneath the pier, you realize something beautiful: The road may end here, but the story doesn't.

You carry it with you, in your heart, in your memories, in the way you see the world now.

Because endings are never just endings. They are beginnings, too.

Route 66 is not just a highway. It's a reminder that adventure belongs to you. Always.

Capture Your Favorite Moments in California

Memory	Route 66 Location	What Happened	Who You Were With	Why It Stuck With You
1				
2				
3				
4				
5				

California Reflection Questions

Endings, Beginnings & Transformation

- What did reaching the Pacific Ocean stir in you?
- Which California moment felt like a celebration or a release?
- How did this final stretch help you reflect on the miles behind you?
- What conversations or memories from this chapter will stay with you?

About the Author

Amy Tarpein is an award-winning accessible travel writer, best-selling author, world-renowned public speaker, advocate, and single mother of ten whose work has transformed how multi-generational families experience the world. With a deep understanding of what it means to travel with a family that doesn't fit the traditional mold, Amy writes with honesty, warmth, and lived experience at the center of every story.

Her journey into advocacy began with her son Elijah, who was born with a rare, terminal brain condition. Determined to show him the world, Amy founded **Elijah's Baby Bucket List**, a movement that has since grown into an internationally recognized force for inclusive tourism. Her mission to make travel possible for families with medically complex children, disabled travelers, caregivers, and an aging society has been featured in national media, including *Woman's Week*, for its impact on reshaping the accessibility landscape.

Amy's work has earned significant recognition, including **two Anthem Awards for Diversity, Equity & Inclusion**, and her platform was named the **Best Accessible Family Travel Blog in the United States for 2025.** Traveling with Elijah, alongside siblings she lovingly calls her *Mini-Humans*, caregivers, and a wide age range of children, taught her a truth she now champions everywhere she goes:

Accessibility isn't a niche topic. It's a universal one. Families with disabled children, aging parents, sensory needs, mobility devices, medical equipment, or simply a desire for gentler travel all deserve to feel welcomed, prepared, and included.

Amy is the author of the best-selling book ***Braver Together, Vol. 1***, where she shares her story of resilience, community, and purpose. Today, she continues to write, speak, and advocate for a world where every family, no matter its size, age range, or needs, can experience the joy of exploration.

When she's not traveling or writing, Amy can be found with a cup/bowl of strong coffee in hand, reminding everyone around her of one of her core life philosophies:

Eat dessert first, joy shouldn't wait!

Acknowledgements

To my children and grandchildren, all of you, thank you for being my greatest teachers, my loudest cheerleaders, and the reason I believe in impossible things. Elijah, you are the heartbeat of this journey. Your courage, your joy, and your way of seeing the world have changed me in ways I will spend my whole life trying to honor.

To Heather, Shannon, Rachel, and Mike, I could not do this without your constant love, encouragement, and unwavering support. Thank you for believing in me every step of the way.

To the families who have trusted me with your stories, thank you. You are the reason I do this work. Your messages, your photos, your questions, your victories, and even your heartbreaks have shaped this book more than you know.

To the caregivers, nurses, therapists, and medical teams who have walked beside us, your compassion has carried us through the hardest days and made the best days possible.

To the destinations, tourism boards, and organizations who believe in accessibility not as a checkbox but as a commitment, thank you for opening your doors wider.

To my community, the parents, advocates, travelers, and friends who show up again and again, your support is the fuel that keeps this movement alive.

And finally, to the Mother Road herself, thank you for reminding me that the world is still full of wonder, and that every family deserves to experience it.

Closing Blessing

A Final Reflection for the Road Ahead

May the road rise to meet you gently.
May the miles unfold with kindness.
May the small towns welcome you like an old friend.
May the neon signs remind you that joy still glows in unexpected places.
May the quiet moments teach you what matters.
May the hard moments show you your strength.
May the laughter of your children echo louder than your worries.
May the world open itself to you fully, generously, beautifully.
And may you always remember that adventure belongs to you, exactly as you are.
The Mother Road doesn't ask you to be fearless. She only asks you to begin.

Apppendix

RESOURCES FOR ACCESSIBLE TRAVEL

These resources are curated specifically for families, caregivers, and travelers navigating mobility devices, medical equipment, sensory needs, and chronic or complex conditions.

Accessible Travel Planning

- **Wheel the World:** Verified accessibility reviews for hotels, attractions, and tours.
- **AccessibleGO** : Community-sourced accessibility insights and travel deals.
- **Open Doors Organization:** Advocacy and resources for accessible tourism.
- **Society for Accessible Travel & Hospitality (SATH):** Education and support for inclusive travel.

Mobility & Equipment

- **Numotion:** Mobility equipment, repairs, and travel support.
- **National Seating & Mobility:** Wheelchairs, seating systems, and equipment solutions.
- **Scootaround:** Mobility rentals delivered to hotels, airports, and attractions.

Air Travel & Transportation

- **TSA Cares:** Assistance for travelers with disabilities or medical needs.
- **Air Carrier Access Act (ACAA):** Your rights when flying with a disability.
- **DOT Disability Hotline:** Support for air travel accessibility issues.

Medical & Emergency Planning

- **MedicAlert Foundation:** Medical IDs and emergency support.
- **Global Rescue:** Emergency evacuation and travel protection.
- **Travelers with Disabilities Act Resources:** Legal protections and guidance.

Sensory-Friendly Travel

- **KultureCity:** Sensory-inclusive certifications and sensory bags.
- **Autism Travel:** Certified autism-friendly destinations and tools.

Community Support

- **Facebook Groups for Accessible Travel**
- **Local disability organizations**
- **Parent and caregiver networks**

Use these resources as tools, not rules. Every family's needs are different, and your journey will be uniquely yours.

PACKING LIST FOR MEDICALLY COMPLEX TRAVEL

This list is designed for families traveling with medical equipment, mobility devices, sensory needs, or chronic conditions. Adjust it to fit your child, your diagnosis, and your comfort level.

Medical Essentials

- Daily medications (plus 2–3 extra days)
- Emergency medications
- Feeding supplies (tubes, syringes, formula, pump)
- Suction machine + extra canisters
- Nebulizer + tubing
- Pulse oximeter + extra probes
- Portable oxygen (if needed)
- Backup batteries + chargers
- Medical binder with care plan
- Copies of prescriptions
- Doctor's letter for travel
- Insurance cards
- Emergency contact list

Mobility & Equipment

- Wheelchair or stroller
- Charger for power chair
- Tools for quick repairs
- Extra straps, cushions, or supports
- Portable ramp (if needed)
- Car-seat or adaptive seating

Comfort & Sensory Items

- Noise-canceling headphones
- Weighted blanket or lap pad
- Fidgets or comfort objects
- Sunglasses or hat

- Snacks and familiar foods
- Extra clothes for spills or sensory needs

Hygiene & Care

- Diapers or briefs
- Wipes
- Disposable pads
- Hand sanitizer
- Gloves
- Trash bags
- Towels or washcloths

Travel Logistics

- Hotel confirmations
- Accessibility notes
- Route planning
- Charging locations
- Emergency stops
- Weather considerations

For the Caregiver

- Water
- Snacks
- Comfortable shoes
- A moment to breathe

This list is not about fear, it's about freedom. Preparation gives you room to enjoy the journey.

ROUTE 66 ACCESSIBILITY CHEAT SHEET

A quick-reference guide for families, caregivers, and travelers with mobility or medical needs.

Illinois

- Chicago attractions: fully accessible
- Museums: elevators + tactile exhibits
- Route 66 icons: mostly level ground
- Drive-in theater: accessible parking

Missouri

- Gateway Arch Museum: fully accessible
- Caves: partial accessibility with staff support
- Neon parks + museums: wide pathways

Kansas

- Short stretch, mostly level
- Bridges + museums: accessible entrances

Oklahoma

- Longest drivable stretch
- Museums: excellent accessibility
- Quirky stops: mostly level terrain

Texas

- Cadillac Ranch: uneven ground after rain
- Big Texan: accessible seating
- Midpoint Café: accessible + cozy

New Mexico

- Santa Fe + Albuquerque: strong accessibility
- Tramway: fully accessible
- Blue Hole: accessible viewing only

Arizona

- Petrified Forest: accessible trails
- Meteor Crater: accessible viewing platforms
- Oatman: level but crowded
- Bearizona: drive-through option

California

- Wigwam Motel: accessible rooms
- Santa Monica Pier: ramps + beach wheelchairs
- Ghost towns: partial accessibility

General Tips

- Call ahead, accessibility varies
- Weather changes terrain
- Carry backup batteries
- Build in rest time
- Trust your instincts

www.ingramcontent.com/pod-product-compliance
Lightning Source LLC
Chambersburg PA
CBHW071321140726
47996CB00005B/1761